Honeymoon Palsy

HONEYMOON PALSY

Poems by
Juliana Gray

Measure Press
Evansville, Indiana

The text of this book is composed in Baskerville.
Composition by R.G.
Manufacturing by Ingram.

Gray, Juliana
   Honeymoon Palsy / by Juliana Gray — 1st ed.

   ISBN-13: 978-1-939574-23-7
   ISBN-10: 1-939574-23-4
   Library of Congress Control Number: 2017913085

Measure Press
526 S. Lincoln Park Dr.
Evansville, IN 47714
http://www.measurepress.com/measure/

Acknowledgments

The author would like to send special thanks and shouts-out to Alfred University; the Sewanee Writers' Conference and my whole Sewanee family; the West Chester University Poetry Conference; La Muse Writers' and Artists' Retreat; my life partner Erica Dawson; my beer and cheese nerds David, Allen, and Dani; lifelong besties Erin McGraw, Andrew Hudgins, and Danny Anderson; my mother, Kay Baggett, and stepfather, Dick Baggett; and my father Jerry Gray, who taught me to love poetry.

Additionally, the author would like to thank the following journals and anthologies in which these poems previously appeared, sometimes in slightly different form.

32 Poems: "House of Sleep" and "Maraschino"
Birmingham Poetry Review: "Lizzie Borden's Pears" and "The Chauffeur's Daughter Recalls Miss Borden"
Blackbird: "Once"
The Book of Scented Things: "*Vanille Abricot Comptoir Sur Pacifique*"
Burrow Press Review: "Action Comics #0"
Cherry Tree: "The Name of Action," "This Vision," "I Take My Leave"
Ducts.org: "Men in the Susquehanna"
Fourteen Hills: "The Domestic"
The Journal: "Letter Written on a Boarding Pass"
Mead: "The Drink"
Measure: "The View from the Trees," "My Crush on Hamlet"
ONE: "Letter Written on a Maple Wing"
PMS: poemmemoirstory: "The Mobled Queen," "Thrift," "Ophelia"
River Styx: "The Story of the Flood" and "The Last Time I Saw Dylan"
Sou'wester: "The Island of Romantic Gestures"
Tupelo Quarterly: "Balthus, *The Victim*, 1946," "My Father's Gun," "Honey Don't"
Unsplendid: "Bounded in a Nutshell"
Yellow Chair Review: "In the Castle of H.H. Holmes"

For Erin and Andrew

CONTENTS

1.

2.

3.

1.

First Ghost

Heaven hadn't been invented yet.
I stood, or thought I stood, beside my brother,

who still clenched the bloody stone as if
he full expected the pile of meat and rags

to give him further argument. Then
I recognized a broken sandal strap,

and knew myself the corpse. I'd never seen
my own face. Now it burbled up

a pulp like rancid pomegranate seeds.
My brother prayed — for himself, as ever —

and bent to gather fallen branches and stones
to conceal the animal thing. I struck at him,

spat, kicked and howled; all passed over,
insubstantial as a dream of rain.

The carcass only half-buried, blood
seeping through the guilty sand, my brother

ran away, sobbing. I remained.
For a time, the wind amused itself,

first covering and then revealing a hand,
a bit of hair, a bone. The beetles came,

and flies; later, jackals. An acacia
sprouted through my ribs, nourished by

my ruined heart. I laughed, or thought I laughed —
my brother was a gardener, after all.

In this way passed the first few lonesome years.
My brothers spread their seed, and the innocent earth

grew thick with people, some of them murderers.
Since then, I have not lacked for company.

How and When

A crash, most likely. Perhaps disease, quick
tendrils of cancer through bone, brain, or breast.
I might decide to hurry myself to rest,
as we're told the poets do — take arsenic,
learn to love a pistol's leaden click,
or slip to sleep with the motor running, my chest
unmoving, cheeks turned rosy. No need for inquest.
I'll leave a note, detectives. Cancel forensics.

Whatever the means, I want my friends to burn
with grief. Even my ex should be very sorry.
Close the casket, kill the carnations, pour
Kentucky bourbon. Beside my father's urn,
make room for mine, or scatter me in Sewanee.
Then wash your hands of me. Close the door.

My Father's Gun

Caliber, I couldn't say,
nor make or model, nor how the grip
settled snug against the palm —
only its ugliness, dark
and squat as a poisonous toad.

Even Dad didn't want it;
holding it, he wore a look
of faint disgust, as if he wished
he were wearing gloves — the face of a man
collecting a dog's steaming pile.

A gift, a thing unwanted, yet
set aside *just in case.*
He tucked it underneath his seat
on long car trips. Just in case?
Of what? The Misfit? *You never know.*

Who gave the gun? His stepfather?
That man who later killed his wife,
my grandmother — shot her, in fact,
and two others — then died in prison,
as my mother often prayed he would?

Can that be right? Who is left to ask?
Clock hands swing like teachers' arms
erasing chalk. I was a child,
learning, studying the gun
in its drawer, when no one else was home.

House of Sleep

The walls still hold; the hardwood floors sigh
like dreaming dogs as the night air cools,
but hold their places firm. Everything —

remote on the coffee table, magazine
opened to a half-read page, one shoe
upon the rug — is just the way you left it,

but turns strange in the blue-green light
of digital clocks. Awakened from a sleep
so complete it might have been your last,

you're baffled, hurt: shouldn't it have collapsed
without you? Isn't this betrayal, the world
simply carrying on so easily?

Empty your bladder; return to your sheeted bier.
Live appliances hum their patient songs,
keeping the nightwatch by cold electric glow.

The Story of the Flood

When Gilgamesh came to the edge of the world,
Utnapishtim the Faraway asked,
"If you are Gilgamesh, why is your face
so starved and burned by wind and sun? Why
is your body unwashed and dressed in stinking skins
of animals? What has brought you here?"

"I am Gilgamesh, king of Uruk,
and why should I not be starved and burned, bereft
of clothing, my body wrapped in stinking skins?
My brother Enkidu, my friend, has died.
He was killed not like a man, in hot battle,
but in wasting sickness sent by jealous gods.
For seven days and nights I wept for him,
until the worms blossomed in his eyes.
He is dead and gone to earth. Help me,
father Utnapishtim, so that I
may bring him back, or never myself die."

Utnapishtim knew this could not be,
but, moved by the hero's grief, offered him
instead a secret: the story of the flood.
He told how years ago, when the stars were young,
the gods grew tired of human noise, and vowed
to send a storm to scour clean the earth.
Yet Utnapishtim, warned in a dream, tore
apart his house of reeds and built a ship,
a mighty barque to shelter his family,

as well as the egg and seed of every beast.
As the rains — gentle, at first — began to fall,
he gathered them: birds of prey and song,
the hooved, the clawed, the legless. He sacrificed
a shining bull as showers turned to tempests.

He told how in the days that followed, he watched
the earth outside his hold, and saw the gods
impaling fathers and sons on lightning spears,
swallowing mothers and daughters in gulping floods.
Soon there was no earth, only the barque
lifted into a sea that bobbed with corpses.
For seven days he watched and wept as the dead,
the bloated meat of his kinsmen, bumped against
his barque of reeds, then sank into the black.
Then Ishtar, Queen of Heaven, looked down and cried,
"What evil have we done? Were these not
our people, our children, and have we not destroyed them?"
She wept down tears of lapis lazuli.

The rest can be quickly told: how the rains
ceased as suddenly as a man can blink,
and Utnapishtim sent a dove to search
for land. Finding none, she returned.
The next day, he sent a swallow; she too
returned. Then he sent a raven, which cawed
from a dry mountaintop, where he beached the barque.
As the waters receded, he made a sacrifice,
and shimmering Ishtar lit upon the deck,
presenting him with one of her lapis tears,
a token of her vow to restore the earth,
and promised that he alone should never die.

"And so, Gilgamesh, you see that none
can live forever, as I have done. Return
to Uruk, and bring this story of the flood,
this secret of the gods, to your people,
and rule in wisdom 'til your days are done."

But Gilgamesh, wrapped in his stinking furs,
wept until the tears cut through the filth
encrusted on his cheeks. Enkidu,
his friend, was dead, never to return.
For Gilgamesh, the world had already ended.

In the Castle
of H.H. Holmes

What's happened to you? How did you get lost?
You'd swear your rented room was down this hall,
but now the corridor seems endless, strange.
The way seemed clear when kindly Mr. Holmes
escorted you this afternoon, but the door
that should have opened on a water closet
reveals a wall of solid brick. Your lamp
casts taunting shadows on stairs that lead to nothing.

Tourist! You came to see America,
four centuries of progress displayed
in a city destroyed by fire and bravely rebuilt,
entirely new. Chicago! The White City!
You trusting fool, you nineteenth-century chump.
You don't know Dahmer, Gacy, or Gein, you don't
know Birkenau, you haven't even read
the stories of Angela Carter. You're unprepared.
You rode the Ferris wheel and almost wept
at the nation's wonders, the coming century.
Watching as you disembarked, a man
in a bowler hat politely shook your hand,
described his newly-built hotel, his "castle,"
located quite nearby, very clean
and modern, designed by the man himself.

So here you are — and there's your room at last!
The door opens on your bags, your clothes
with complicated Victorian clasps and stays,
the sweet familiar things you love because
you don't know any better. You hear a key
inserted in the lock, the tumblers' fall.
The spigot's hidden, but you smell the gas.
Soon you'll wake in the Castle basement, strapped
to the stretching rack. If you crane your neck, you'll see
the skeletons, some of them not yet clean,
that will be sold to doctors and medical schools
that don't ask questions. Your guide, Mr. Holmes,
will greet you, doffing his hat, softly explaining
exactly what he's about to do to you.
You'll never drive a car, use a zipper,
listen to Billie Holiday moan
through a radio. A secret door
is sliding open in the wall. You'll see
the brave new future, the thing you came here for.

Balthus, *The Victim*, 1946

Where does the greedy eye come to rest?
The girl unfolds on the soiled white sheet,

her skin as gray-flecked as wartime bread.
Hard to look at her face, her parted lips,

for longer than a moment; hard not to stare
at her smooth, demure cunt, the dead center

of the canvas. Balthus leads the eye from left,
along the awkward splay of her foot, right

and down the calf, the knee's violent turn,
up the rounded thigh to the bare plane

of stomach, chest, dangling arm, the hand
that may be holding onto something small.

Her eyes are closed, or mostly closed. Perhaps
she's only sleeping. Her body is unmarked,

unbloodied; only her ear is slightly red,
as if the neighbors have been gossiping.

If she's asleep or in a trance, then why
the title? Why, below her puzzling face,

underneath the exposed, ugly mattress,
has Balthus dropped on the floor a spotless knife?

The blade points toward the victim's heart.
The haft — one of us must pick it up.

Miss Emma Borden
Visits Her Sister in Jail

Double rows of six silver eyelets,
strung with black laces, on each of my shoes.
One window with one ugly lock.
Twelve roses linking vines around
my teacup's rim, ten and an orphaned petal
on the saucer, which was chipped and dirty.
When Lizzie, sulking, refused to speak to me,
I counted up the prison matron's room:
two Bibles, one tempting deck of cards,
one table, one threadbare woolen rug, one door.
Twenty days since our parents' murders.

That morning, when I came to sit with her,
Lizzie threw herself upon the couch
and sobbed that I had given her away.
"No, never!" I cried. "And how could I,
when you are innocent?" In the next room,
the matron, whose room Lizzie occupied,
was listening. Anyone could hear.
Lizzie, sniffling, turned her back to me;
I drew near the single wooden chair
and stroked her arm, her skin burning hot
beneath the black mourning rags. Poor girl,
she'd been the one to find our father killed,
chopped to bits like a block of party ice.
I wonder that she didn't swoon; I'm sure

I would have, had I been at home that day.
Our stepmother lying dead upstairs,
Father below, the stifling August heat —
the house still reeked of blood when I came home.
Lizzie had closed all the windows and curtains
against the gawkers and sat in the parlor with friends,
discussing undertakers, eating cake.

And yet today, her strength seemed to fail.
Mrs. Reagan bustled about, pretending
to tidy up the room, chatting with Lizzie.
I was counting fringes on the rug
when her voice turned sly. "There's one simple thing,
Miss Borden, I wager you cannot do."
"Indeed? And what is that?" Lizzie chirped.
"Break an egg."
                Lizzie looked insulted.
"Mrs. Reagan, I can break an egg."
"Not the way I'd have you do it." The crone
licked her dry lips. "Will you bet
a dollar?"
                "A quarter."
                        The matron hurried off
to fetch the egg. When her footsteps faded, I hissed,
"Lizzie, what are you doing? You cannot gamble
when you are in prison, soon to be on trial
for your life!"
                She smoothed her dress. "It's just a game,
Emma, to pass the time. You worry too much."

Mrs. Reagan was back in a blink — she must
have had the wager planned — carrying

a speckled egg. She had Lizzie stand
away from me, in case she "broke it wrong"
and egg would stain my dress. "Hold it thus,
in your right hand, and squeeze as hard as you can."
Lizzie took the egg, smirked at me,
and folded her long fingers over it.
Her knuckles whitened, the cords of her wrist popped up,
but the egg remained whole. Lizzie stood
straight, drew a manly breath, and squeezed
as if to crush the life that never was
from the innocent egg. Then she opened her hand
and almost threw the pale, uncracked thing
at Mrs. Reagan. The woman caught it, barely.
I knew Lizzie was angry, but she sounded cheerful
when she said, "That is the first thing
I undertook to do that I never could."
I paid the matron; both coin and egg vanished
in her pockets. She'd boil it for her supper,
probably. I hoped she'd choke on it.
My sister calmly smiled, fixed her eyes
on a vacant spot just above our heads,
and gently folded her unblemished hands.

Action Comics #0

Infinite space, infinite worlds, some
of them inhabited by beings wise
enough to apprehend their planet's doom.
What to save? How to eulogize
a world before it shudders into ash?
Alien parents tuck their dearest pearl
into a pod, a rocket, a crystal crèche
and launch it into hopeful space. The girl
or boy or multi-gendered child inside
dies in hypersleep; the fuel depletes;
life support malfunctions; the ship collides
with a random bit of hurtling debris.
An orphanage of coffins crowds the sky.
Still, Jor-El and Lara have to try.

The View from the Trees

For hours, the plumber's quiet son — all knees,
knobby elbows, and yes-ma'am manners —
has fetched from his father's truck great hammers
and wrenches. Now, sniffling with allergies
to my cats, he waits in the truck and studies the trees.
Skinny thing, shy with an awkward stammer,
he wipes his nose with a red bandanna
and whistles lonesome calls to wrens and phoebes.

I'm slipping into the old familiar snare,
projecting myself into this depiction
like the worst kind of navel-gazing hack.
Why not write the boy as happy, there
in the tender shade? All of this is fiction,
and sometimes the curious birds whistle back.

Men in the Susquehanna

Below the overpass, a dozen men
are staggered like a mean bowling split
across the shining flats. How can these men
be here on a Wednesday morning, fishing for trout?
Perhaps they've taken the day off from work.
Perhaps they don't have work. They gritted their teeth
all winter long, but now they take up hope
of plenty, fresh fillets on the grill or fried
in popping bacon grease, a freezer full
enough to last 'til spring turkey season.

Better to think of it as a holiday,
the men luxurious in new waders,
expensive flies and reels. They must hold rods;
driving past, I only see their trunks
dark and surely cold in April water
that gleams like foil, these men who stand so still,
waiting, terrified, to feel the catch
of some great, unbearable hook.

In Hunting Season

A deer, almost certainly a deer,
that heavy shape collapsed where lawn gives way

to snowy woods. Last night the waxing moon
made the yard a blank, glowing page,

where now this shape has signed its testament.
The body curves like a child in sleep. Too big

for a dog. It wears on its back a trifling dust
of snow, like sugar sifted over cake.

A hunter must have wounded it, lost
the trail as it stumbled over the village line.

A bad kill, a shame, my friend would say.
Fred's a hunter and biologist;

he takes a careful aim. Last year his dog
came whining to the door, limping, bleeding

from a wound in his flank. The bullet passed
clean through, the vet told my friend, who rubbed

his dog's ears, called him good boy.
At a local dive, he parked beside the truck

he'd seen several times near his land.
Fred's a gentle man, tender when

he bands a songbird's leg. He asked, politely,
who drove the truck. The bartender flicked her eyes

away; the camo-coated men anchored
down their stools, studied warm Labatts.

Even with Fred's beard and flannel, they smelled
the college on him. "I just want to know,"

he said, louder than he meant, "which
of you motherfuckers shot my dog."

It could have gotten ugly. Instead, my friend
returned home, to his daughter and little son.

The dog — his name is Blitz — recovered, though he
was shy of the woods and strangers for a while.

A good dog. Here, the twisted shape
beside the spruce is larger, though not by much.

A hunter will be coming for it soon,
across the creek on the makeshift wooden bridge

the neighbor children built. The carcass must
be valuable to someone. A man will come

in heavy boots, looking for meat, for trophy.

The Last Time I Saw Dylan

He looked like Vincent Price: black
suit, pencil mustache, his voice
a raven's croak. If he still loved
performing, he kept it secret, blowing
his harmonica with his back turned
to the audience. He sounded awful,

really, and I expected awful.
His white hat cast wings of black
across his eyes as he slowly turned
to the piano and dragged his voice
through "Simple Twist of Fate," blowing
the lyrics, wrecking the song I loved.

Inheriting my father's love
for Dylan, I grew up full of awe
of every holy note of "Blowing
in the Wind." The pristine black
vinyl of Dad's collection turned,
and we'd listen together to that voice.

Even then, Dylan's voice
wasn't pretty, but I learned to love
the rasps and burrs, the way he turned
not just love but pain, an awful
lonesomeness, to pure black
lines of poetry, blowing

like the western wind, blowing
an idiot wind. My father's voice
when I called about the show was black
with envy — he said he would have loved
to see the concert with me, awful
as it was. The years have turned.

My father is dead, and Dylan's turned
out another album, blowing
the critics away. How sad and awful
to hear those songs, that voice
and not the other voice I loved,
burned away to ashes black.

If he returned, he would have loved
the Duquesne whistle's blowing, the voice
an awful mourner's rag of black.

2.

"Why should we in our peevish opposition,
Take it to heart? Fie, 'tis a fault to heaven,
A fault against the dead, a fault to nature,
To reason most absurd, whose common theme
Is death of fathers . . . ."
  — *Hamlet* Act I, Scene 2

The Mobled Queen

From what honey-drenched dreams she woke,
I cannot say; nor how long she clenched
her bridegroom to her breast before she felt
his sandbag weight, his slowly cooling skin.
She ran, looking half a ghost herself
in her white gown — ran barefoot up and down
the hall, knocking on the hotel doors.
Frantic as Sue was, her knocks were soft;
even then she hated to wake the guests
so early. Her wedding dress the night before
had been the color of champagne, but now,
as I walk out and she whispers, "I can't wake up
your father," her widow's streaming gown is white.

Thrift

"Indeed, my lord, it followed hard upon."

We shower, make tearful calls, delay
as long as we can, then drive to Sue's to mourn
with strangers, our unfamiliar family.
Already the well-wishing mob has landed
with food, plastic cups, a cooler of ice,
as if tailgating for a losing team.
Beside the pulled pork, buns, and slaw
left over from the wedding eve's party,
sit casseroles, chunks of watermelon,
four store-bought tubs of potato salad,
an oblong box of Publix fried chicken.
Already I am sick of *sorry*. I drink
a beer, hold a plate of cold shrimp
(another leftover), thinking if my hands
are kept full, no one will try to hug me.
Already I am sick. Some chatty woman
reads the labels. *New York Potato Salad?*
You're from New York, aren't you? What makes
it New York style? I'm from Alabama.
I don't know. I've never heard of that
before. No, I live a long way
from the city, five hours' drive, the country,
my father wed last night and died this morning,
I don't know you people, I don't know.

Ophelia

One role my sister never played, though once
she scrubbed at her hands on the most depressing stage
in Atlanta. When she cried, "Out, out!," I hoped
it was my cue to leave. But afterward,
waiting for the Lady in the lobby,
Dad looked wistful and said, "I know I'm biased,
but I think she was the best thing in the play."
I bit my cheek — *there was a best thing?* —
and clutched the congratulatory roses we'd bought.

Now her grief is real. She struts and frets
across Dad's empty patio, smoking,
drinking wine, pouring into her phone
some sad soliloquy I can't hear.
Through the kitchen window I see her pace,
sobbing, her red hair streaming mermaid-like.
Her fingers tremble around her glass. She lifts
it high and hurls it down, another smashed
to shards, so everyone can see she's drowning.

All My Mirth

Suddenly my fashion sense is nonsense:
skulls on t-shirts, skulls on flip-flops, skulls
on bracelets, necklaces. On my favorite tee,
a death's head grins, "I live inside your face!"
That skull had a tongue in it, and could sing once.
Back into the closet, behind the arras;
that's nothing to wear to the new widow's house.

Without my gallows humor, my irony,
I'm mute, unarmed. *What was the 'something blue'*
at last night's wedding? My father's face. Be quiet.
Be nice, for once. *What do you call a man*
who gets married and dies the next day?
There's nothing I can say. Bite your tongue.
Where be your gibes now? They call him lucky.

To Sleep, Perchance

"'Tis given out that, sleeping in my orchard,
A serpent stung me."

Not poison, we suspect, but omissions, lies:
some secret diagnosis he hadn't told.
An hour after leaving the emergency room,
I rifle his bathroom drawers, gather the pills,
but find, at worst, empty Viagra tubes,
anti-depressants, nothing for heart or cancer.

Yet the bride and widow wants an answer.
An autopsy returns with wicked speed:
he died, it says, of sleep apnea,
his system clear of drugs: a verdict meant
to stop our guilty tears. But I can't rest.
Have I not eyes? Did I not see the wine,
champagne, scotch and satisfied cigars?
Did Sue not blame herself for giving him
a Xanax when they went to bed? He asked
his wife because he forgot to pack his own;
he took one every night to help him sleep.
Oh, to sleep. How can the body stop
its breathing, slow the thin and wholesome blood
and drift into that night without a sunrise?
How can a sleeper fail to wake? He gave
a funny kind of snore, she said; but then,
he always snored. I wish for serpents, poison,
a villain to deserve my swift revenge.

The Name of Action

"I am not Prince Hamlet, nor was meant to be."

We start with the fridge, the one I swear I cleaned
of expired food every year at Christmas;
yet rancid salsas, slowly softening olives,
cheeses old enough for kindergarten
fill the Hefty bags. We freshen drinks,
tackle the cabinets, the chest of drawers,
open the closets and turn, horrified.
"Was Dad a hoarder?" "Who needs a giant bin
of cashmere sweaters in fucking *Georgia*?" No one,
not even him; the tags are still attached.

After my sister leaves, I keep going,
filling bags with magazines, socks
too worn to donate, snapshots of former girlfriends
I don't want Sue to find. Bourbon and ginger
suffice til the flat ginger ale runs out;
then Maker's on the rocks, the empty bottle
added to the trash. I can almost curse him,
staring down the bins of light bulbs, bins
of tote bags, batteries, papers, extension cords.

My father, I am ill at these numbers:
21 toothpastes, 14 floss,
16 brushes, all new, boxed
and set aside for the battered women's shelter;
18 sacks of sport coats, pants, shirts
for Goodwill to pick up; 160
DVDs dropped at the public library;

dozens of trash bags I dragged to the curb.
This quantity of love makes up my sum,
so I can tell whoever asks, *look,*
I did something, everything I could.

The Drink

"They clepe us drunkards . . . ."

Whatever's open has to go: brandy,
weird liqueurs, curdled Irish creams
flush down the kitchen sink. It's criminal
to mix Bombay Sapphire with tonic, but this
is no martini party, and the days are long.
Irish coffee in the mornings, beer
at lunch, gin and juice (a felony!)
all afternoon, then vodka, bourbon, wine —
we tell ourselves we're helping, emptying
his cabinets, this is part of the work.

So, it seems, is draining Pimm's cups
with Sue's anxious daughters, margaritas
and tequila shots after the visitation.
At the funeral home, I fall half in love
with one of our new step-brothers-in-law
who pulls from his car a fifth of Makers Mark
and a cooler of ice. We toast the old man
in the parking lot, agree he would approve.

The night of the wedding, I bought a six-pack,
something cold to sip while I dressed,
and found Dad pacing the hotel lobby,
sweetly nervous. I laughed and gave him a beer.
It was the last time I saw him alone.
That morning, as paramedics rolled him out,
I found the beer, its brown bottle warm
where he'd left it, still full, untouched.

This Vision

"He seemed to find his way without his eyes,
For out o'doors he went without their helps . . . ."

We learned to ask before we left the car,
or as we crossed the parking lot: "Dad,
do you have your glasses?" If he forgot, then we
were doomed to reading aloud the wine lists, menus,
price tags, theater times. "Wait, go back.
What was on the roasted duck again?
Did you say there was a pinot gris?"
His house acquired a coat of fur and grime
he couldn't see; my sister and I would clean
discreetly when we visited, sweeping
floors and scrubbing toilets while he slept.
"I never needed glasses," he bragged, "until
I turned forty, and then I went straight
to bifocals. The same will happen to you."

Now we find his glasses everywhere.
Seven pairs, ten, thirteen — they fill
the basket we've set out to collect them all.
The Lions Club recycles them, gives
them to the poor. Already his corneas,
the only organs we were asked to donate,
must have been transplanted. We act as if
they help, these easy little charities.
"Dad would have wanted it this way."
Remember me. We act as if we see.

The Lady

"Both here and hence pursue me lasting strife,
If, once a widow, ever I be wife!"

We'd learned not to take them seriously,
our father's girlfriends. After thirty years —

how many bitter? he never said — of marriage
to our mother, we couldn't blame the man

for having fun. We met so many blondes
with French manicures and brittle laughs.

They'd drop by for a glass of wine or three,
tell outrageous stories, confide when Dad

had left the room that he was really special.
Smart ladies, they knew they had to win

the daughters. We hardly ever met one twice.
But Sue came back, and when she gave him shit,

we saw how much he loved it. She was a widow,
Dad said, her husband retired Air Force. One day,

while raking leaves, a strange countenance
(*more in sorrow than in anger*) crossed

her husband's face. He dropped to the ground at her feet.
A stroke, maybe, Dad said. She's still haunted.

The perfect woman, then, to never marry
our father. We thought we had it figured out.

But in the hazy days between the wedding
and funeral, between two preachers

and formal dresses, Sue told us that Dad
proposed to her almost as soon as they met,

and every few months thereafter. She told him no,
no, she wasn't ready, then finally yes.

The Player King admits, *'Tis not strange*
that even our loves should with our fortunes change.

I find, tucked inside a file, a printout
Dad had saved for years: a dating profile

of a hesitant widow, her hobbies, likes and dislikes,
her picture taken by an encouraging friend.

The bottle blonde shyly smiles from the page —
a haunted woman, ready to take a chance.

I Take My Leave

"Thus set it down: he shall with speed to England . . . ."

If there were living batteries in the clocks,
they'd strike the hour. Time for me to go.
My car is packed with stuff: CDs, books,
a set of wine glasses, unopened scotch,
family photographs released from frames.
A portrait of Dad, bright acrylic paint
on cardboard, I'd made when I was maybe ten,
he'd hung in his living room. Things like this
will have to wait for someone after me,
going through my empty, unhaunted house,
to find them meaningless and throw them out.
I'll store it in a box.

                    Wrapped in socks
in a suitcase corner, a tiny cedar urn,
identical to my sister's and the best man's,
a miniature of Sue's. In the same bag,
a wine stopper topped with a heart of glass,
the wedding keepsake, one for every guest.
Penetrable stuff, flat and dull.
Time to go. Maybe the long drive
and Northern landscapes different shall expel
this something-settled matter in my heart.
It won't, of course. One last souvenir
is stowed away: the little wooden chair
he sat on as a boy, skinny and poor.
He saved it from his murdered mother's house,
years ago. That's where he sat, eating

suppers of peas and cornbread, reading about the Hardy Boys and Tarzan, dreaming of Mars, Africa, undiscovered countries.

The Ghost

"My father, methinks I see my father."

Not in the house, all but empty now
and priced to sell; not in the household stuff
I've driven home, movies, music, knives;
not in the photographs, scallop-edged,
of family whose names I never learned;
not even in the little wooden urn,
my share of ashes, high upon my shelf.

The modern ghost is doomed to walk the web.
In picture galleries of the wedding night,
he smiles at his bride, at me behind the lens.
On Facebook — what a falling-off was there! —
below the condolences, his final update:
"Today is my wedding day. I'm a lucky man!"
O my ironic soul. O cursed spite.

Questions

*"Glean what afflicts him. . . . Question and answer. Old
ways are the best ways."*

What did Sue say to you in the hotel hallway?
    "I can't wake up your father."
What did you do?
    Everything I could.
What did you do?
    *Wheeled my luggage to their door, left it in the hall,
    went inside, saw him on the bed. Called his name.*
You barely touched him, just gave his shoulder
half a shake. Why didn't you try CPR?
    He was naked. It was his wedding night.
Why did you run all the way to the front desk
to call the ambulance? There was a phone
in the room. You had a cell.
    My father's face was blue.
All that running, through the lobby,
through the little breakfast nook,
families making their own waffles
as you tore past. Why did you do that?
    I ran.
Were you crying?
    I ran.
What's the last thing you did before you left your room?
    I wrote a note to leave on the windshield of Dad's car.
What did it say?
    "Congratulations, and have fun in Hilton Head!" Their honeymoon.
What happened to the note?
    I found it in my purse, weeks later. I'd tucked it in a pocket.

What did you do?

I cried. I ran. I didn't cry. Because I knew that he was gone.

Bounded in a Nutshell

Late August, lying with a book
upon the sofa — what the summer should
have been. I'm trying to hold what's left of it.
My novel, too, is near its end, and so
I lie past comfort with the obese cat
atop my chest, trying to ignore
the yells of neighbor kids playing outside.

There. Put down the book, break the spell,
stare away at nothing — except my eyes
come to rest on the tiny wooden urn,
glossy and acorn-shaped, high on the shelf
where I haven't looked for a month. My share of ashes.
"He's not in that box," I said at the service;
so why am I crying now? I haven't opened
the urn, untwisted its cap. Is there a bag
inside? Is it sealed? Or are they loose,
sifting and reshaping like miniature dunes
each time I walk past, my head turned?
Why, why won't those children stop screaming?

Epithalamion

"Those that are married already — all but one — shall live."

And there it was: heavy cardstock embossed
with honey-golden fleurs-de-lis, swirls
of script, and the killer detail: a champagne bow
tied like a satin noose across their names.
"A bow!" I ranted to friends. "Who puts a bow
on invitations to a second wedding!
He's sixty-nine! Why get married now?"
I pouted and huffed, complained, refused to buy
a new dress or heels, mocked the restaurant's
web site and menu ("the best in Macon!").
Yes, I behaved badly. In my heart
there was a kind of fighting that would not let
me sleep. Yes, it hurts to think of it now —

Now, putting the invitation (its bow
a little crushed from months in a file) aside,
refilling my mug of tea, listening
to music loud enough to rattle the walls —
an autumn Saturday, drawn on to pleasures.
We might have happily wasted such a day
on football, movies, cooking a buttery meal.
"You're too young to live alone forever,"
he told me just after my divorce.
But there's a kind of joy in selfishness.
Yes, I wanted no more marriages —
not that second love must needs be treason,
or second wife be cursed — I thought we shared
the love of solitude. He wanted love.

Words, words, words. Enter the Players
as husband and wife, holding hands, posing
for pictures with friends. The champagne fleurs-de-lis
have reappeared on damasked table settings
that match the bridal dress, our bubbling toasts.
They kiss and feed each other cake, a taste
of sweetness, and I do believe that they're in love.
We drink to love until my glass is empty,
then refill it, drink again, to love.
Sinatra croons "The Best is Yet to Come."
My father lives for one more night, the best
he could have wished for. The dumb show follows.

3.

Honeymoon Palsy

After fumblings they call "making love,"
the newlywed couple spoons, a pose
they've seen in movies: hand on breast, his nose
buried in her hair, his arm shoved
beneath her head. The tender weight above
his arm seems nothing, so he sleeps, enclosed
in bliss, the afterglow's sweet repose.
He wakes to a hand dead as a pitcher's glove.

Usually, the damaged nerve recovers.
Throughout the long, oblivious nights, they lie,
seemingly aligned, heart to heart.
Already, they've learned so much, these new lovers:
touching without meeting the other's eye,
going numb to each other, part by part.

The Island
of Romantic Gestures

Call it a quirk of lovestruck currents, a gyre
swirling itself into a watery heart.

Whatever its scientific origin,
here's where keepsakes cast into the sea

eventually end. Every letter
scattered from a bridge, snapshot dropped

over a ferry's rail, nostalgic token
flung, strewn or slipped into waves

frothed like soft meringue — they arrive
here, beached on black volcanic sand.

See the bits of paper underfoot?
Vacation postcards and perfumed stationery,

the sweetest compost, enrich the dunes — look
how beachgrass grows as thick as the devil's whiskers.

Albatrosses line their shallow nests
with shreds of neckties, scarves, unraveled threads

from boyfriends' t-shirts stolen for pajamas.
Turtle hatchlings rarely make their way

from nest to sea without becoming snagged
on tarnished jewelry; when they return

to lay their own clutches, moonlight sparks
on broken lockets and links of silver chain

embedded in their shells. Some are choked
by golden rings; the currents bring their bodies

back to shore. Look there, those ivory shards.
The suicides are ground to little more

than half-dressed skeletons by the time
the tides bear them here; the natives carve

their femurs into flutes, make knotty blossoms
of vertebrae. Our only industry

is mordant scrimshaw; that, and the odd tourist
like yourself. No, I do not know

your poet Crane, but if he killed himself
for love, his body must have drifted here.

But no, you won't find any poisoned husbands
or wives dumped with weights tied to wrists

and broken necks; no unwanted babes
drowned or set adrift, still wailing,

come to rest upon our humble strand.
Murders are the next island over.

Honey Don't

He gave me a drink. He gave me a ring
and a cigarette, and I gave it back.
I wanted his hands. He gave me
a clock. I wanted skin.
He gave me paper tickets, paper cards.
He gave me a cotton dress, soap
shaped like rocks, rocks shaped like soap,
a little tray to set them on.
He gave me a belt, and I gave it back.
I wanted flesh. He gave me a peach.
I wanted a door. He gave me a door.
By then, I wanted blood.
He gave me licorice. He gave me a drink.
I wanted his hand on my throat.
He gave me copper wind chimes,
blithely tinkling in the hurricane.

My Crush on Hamlet

He's just the dreamiest: young, depressed,
a student carrying a book (unread)
in every tortured scene, always dressed
in black. I love when he wishes he were dead,
or had never been born at all. I love the vows,
how all those words dissolve to candyfloss
the instant that the time to act is "now."
Oh, he's just my type! — self-pity, pathos,
an overbearing mom! He'll never state
"I love you" till his girlfriend's in the ground.
He'll never make his father proud, or rate
succession, either to manhood or the crown.
There'll be no happy ending to the tale.
Again and again, I get to watch him fail.

Obscene Poem, Not to Be Read

Fresh-cut okra smells like semen. There,
I've said it. I never slice those tender spears,

their innocent slime clinging to my knife,
without recalling old lovers. Please

don't tell my mother I wrote this. Vulgar, she'd say.
She'd flinch at "lovers," the stark plurality.

But here's this brown, hairy chestnut husk,
picked up along a village road in France,

that can't help but be a little cunt.
I'm sorry, Mom. I tried to make it seem

a sea urchin, or a bearded man's mouth,
but that's just another joke for pussy,

and here's this prickly thing, split wide
into four velvety lobes, catspaw-soft

inside, the cup that held the glossy fruit.
My mother taught me how to fry okra.

I love my dull mother. I honestly do.
When counting lovers, I need both hands.

The Chauffeur's Daughter
Recalls Miss Borden

Papa said that I must curtsey, hide
my dirty nails, address her as Miss Borden
or Miss Lisbeth — never Lizzie, for she
had changed it after the unpleasantness.
I was good, and so Papa let me sit
in Miss Borden's Buick in her garage;
slowly the turntable would spin, the motor
grinding like an angry giant's teeth,
and the car would swing from back to front,
ready for Papa to take it out again.
I was allowed to touch the wheel, but not
the pedals as I pretended to drive Miss Borden
through town, her Boston terrier happily panting
beside her, top down, on our way
to Oak Grove Cemetery to visit her father.

Mama didn't like me to talk to her,
but Miss Borden was always kind. She'd stand
on the back porch of Maplecroft and feed
the birds and squirrels, coaxing them ever nearer
until the squirrels climbed upon her shoulders
to nibble seeds she'd trailed along her silks.
She gave me cookies, though she was no baker;
I preferred the foil-wrapped peppermints
she kept in a candy dish beside the door.
She always pressed a couple into my hand

after letting me visit her canaries,
pretty as daffodils in their parlor cages.

When Mama and Papa thought I'd gone to sleep,
I'd hear them talking. "The people of this town
have evil minds," my Papa said, and told
how when he drove Miss Borden to Wilmot's to buy
some record needles, the customers and help
would gather on the balcony to watch her.
Mama protested mildly — there must be
a reason, mustn't there, why Miss Emma
refused to live with her sister anymore?
And never visited from Newmarket?
And what about that actress, Miss O'Neill?
"You can't deny, Henry, that wasn't proper.
You saw the empty liquor bottles — who knows
what else was going on inside that house?"
What could she mean? I'd puzzle at her words
until I fell asleep.

       Miss Borden died
of pneumonia, and was buried at her father's feet
as she'd requested. Although the probate lingers,
we know her generous gifts: three thousand
to each of her longtime servants, including Papa;
money and jewelry to friends, a large bequest
to the Animal Rescue League, to benefit
the creatures that keep their silence. Even I
was named in the will, with a gift of two thousand
that Papa says he will invest for me
until I'm married. After the funeral,
sipping a cup of tea, Mama said,

"It was good of so many to pay their respects."
"Respect!" Papa barked. "More like revenge.
And now she's gone, what will the gossips eat
for supper?" Mama flicked her eyes at me,
and I went into the yard. A squirrel chittered,
scolding me for coming empty-handed.
I leaned against the tree, kicked the bark.
How could people tell such tales, repeat
that hateful rhyme? If she were capable,
the lady who loved her horses and little dogs —
if she could bury such a crime within
a wicked heart, then so might anyone!

Trompe L'oeil

A row of windows in dirty casements, sills
jammed with bottles, vases, impoverished plants

stuck between the glass and shoddy drapes,
each cracked or fastened sash signaling

the choice between a spring Parisian breeze
or sealed silence against the autoroute —

and at the end, this larger portal, bright
with yellow curtains, geraniums, a cat

curled beneath a woman's resting hand.
Her other hand supports her teacup chin;

in her blue dress, her bobbed reddish hair,
her distant look of what might be mild arousal

or a stomach ache, she seems the Paris vision
the artist must have wished for, compelling him

to lean out with his pot and brush, reaching
like a burglar from his window to hers.

Her head's a bit too large, her mouth askew.
She wants something better, too — music,

light, a lover who's a proper artist.
She sees him now, walking toward the flat.

She smiles; he hasn't forgotten to bring the wine
she asked for this morning, the requisite loaf of bread.

Letter Written on a Boarding Pass

I stole your trick, a dab of Dijon whisked
into the scrambled eggs, yellow to yellow,
a little tang. I will not give you credit.
Out back, scratched in snow, a wallow
where deer have slept. You grind your teeth at night.
Let's fuck. Let's eat too much ice cream.
Let's walk the dog. You can dim the light.
Let's finally watch *Heaven's Gate*, the scene
where fresh-faced students twirl their ladies' skirts
on the lawn, the scene where lovers skate a gyre
on ice laid thick like fondant over dirt,
the scene where everything is on fire.
Make me a drink. Show me how to start
this letter: *dear friend, dear no one, dear heart.*

Maraschino

Means, *liqueur distilled from small, black*
mascara cherries. Means, *cherries preserved*
in that liqueur. Means, *this is going to hurt.*
Rainiers, Golds, plump Royal Annes
are soaked in brine, bleached like bloodstained clothes
in calcium chloride and reeking sulfur dioxide
until their brightness leaches out and skins
are plasticized to snap between the teeth.
They steep in great vats of sweet dye,
red as Valentines and deadly toads,
swirling cold in a slow centrifuge
of sickly red.
          And here's the handsome man
who calls you *sugar*, calls you other things
when the lights are out, shaking a frosted bullet
of bourbon, vermouth, bitters, shattered ice.
He strains it into a cone-shaped glass that holds
a single maraschino, poison-bright.
It drowns in amber, bumps against the glass.
Yes, he expects you to eat it, even as
it settles like an excised lump preserved
for biopsy. He expects you to put on lipstick,
take the cherry whole into your mouth,
and work your tongue until you've tied the stem
into an impossible knot. Take your time.
He'll watch you do it. He can wait all night,
even if it takes the whole damn jar.

Bewitched

First the wine glasses wouldn't fit
in the dishwasher. Their crystal stems snapped
lightly as the legs of thoroughbreds.
Then the china — the fussy, frumpy pattern
you picked because you thought *traditional*
meant *adult* — those ugly gold-rimmed plates
sparked alarmingly to life in the microwave.

Your registry has set you up to fail.
Who did you think you'd be, the woman who
nibbled from a golden salad plate
and sipped merlot from a hand-washed glass?
You're a sitcom housewife, smart and sassy,
zipped inside a polyester dress,
breathing teaspoons as she mixes drinks.
Her husband needs a double — he's exhausted,
the boss doesn't listen to his ideas,
and that's why the husband has invited him
to dinner, which she must conjure in an hour
and serve with a twinkling smile. That old show.

And now, the cake is burning. The roast is raw.
You're wearing yoga pants and drinking beer,
flour smeared across your widening ass,
while your husband — who looks suddenly strange,
almost like a different man, except
for his disappointment — takes his drink and leaves
the room. You sniff; flour tickles your nose,

makes it twitch. He won't yet say the words
you hear — *I never should have married that witch.*

Morning Run
Past Student Dorms

Through rows of windows open to admit
whirring box fans and needles of eastern light,
I see their standard bedsteads, pillows, a bit
of shoulder, the crown of a head still dreaming midnight.
The beds are awful — I remember — small
and hard, with plastic covers that make you sweat
and bunch the sheets, backed against a wall,
tossing for air, kicking the posts. And yet,
so many of these narrow beds are shared,
two bodies spooning, pressing silently
to spare the roommate's sleep, two heads paired
on the pillow; in one of their rooms, a vacancy.
Such carelessness. It used to all mean more.
Neglected alarms are singing to the floor.

The Domestic

Here's the bowerbird, erecting his apse
of sticks, devoting hours of his short life
to decorating the nest with snails, glass,
buttons, bits of blue plastic or tin,
shining car keys, spent rifle shells.

Sharp-eyed cormorants of Labrador
comb the beach for shipwrecks, line their nests
with salvaged hairpins, combs, pocketknives.
Ravens in Chihuahua lay their eggs,
their animal hopes, in snarls of barbed wire.

How cleverly the birds adapt themselves,
fit their domestic drive to a world of trash
and find it beautiful. They lure a mate
with needles, bed their children in fiberglass.
Under the eaves of a Lincolnshire shop, sparrows

lined their nests with cast-off cigarettes,
one, at least, still smoldering. The shop
went up in pretty flames; the birds survived.
The birds are makers, artists of the air.
Humans teach them how to burn.

Vanille Abricot Comptoir Sud Pacifique

I've never been sweet, but two dabs
behind the ear, and I'm a sugar cookie,
a walking confection, light as vanilla meringue.

I strolled downtown, past a park where children
abandoned slides, tumbled like chimpanzees
from the jungle gym, begging their mothers for candy.

The ice cream parlors were mobbed for tutti frutti.
The bakeries sold out of snickerdoodles,
shortbread, ladyfingers, then barred their doors.

I had a craving, too, so stepped inside
a hipster bar. The patrons' nostrils flared;
they tossed their PBRs and ordered rounds

of craft cocktails with muddled apricot,
agave nectar, blood oranges,
vermouth and local cider. Their jaws ached

for a taste of me. One skinny boy
followed my trail, through the town gone mad
for sweetness, back to my cottage in the woods.

He told me his name as I peeled away his jeans,
but I just called him Hansel. The skinny boys
are all called Hansel, and they fatten up just fine.

Lizzie Borden's Pears

In spring, the smell drove her mad.
Those blossoms, airy as lace, stank
of fish and rot and something else;

she'd heard the neighbor boys snicker,
passing by. She locked the casements
until the white petals browned

and fell, displaced by hard, ungrateful fruits.
Then, the days were hot. She raised
her bedroom windows, prayed for breeze.

That air, impossible to breathe —
she could find no relief from it.
The ripened pears dropped to earth.

At night, their thuds brought restless dreams
of strange men lurking in the yard.
She woke each morning drenched in sweat.

She was often ill that summer.
Everyone was ill. The meat
went bad in a day, cakes turned sour,

her parents retched their dinners at night,
then breakfasted on leftovers.
That morning, Lizzie could not eat,

could not abide even the smell
of johnnycakes and mutton stew.
She fled into the barn loft,

taking an apron full of pears.
There, she said, she sat and ate
for twenty or thirty minutes — she wolfed

her alibi pears to the cores.
Perhaps she thought of Saint Augustine,
who in his youth stole his neighbor's pears,

not for joy or hunger, but merely sin.
Inside the house, the air had changed.
Smell of iron. Soft grains.

Letter Written
on a Maple Wing

At last, I've mastered patience.
      Look how slowly, since you left,
            I have befriended the birds.

Feeders ring the yard,
      thistle and suet for the taking.
            Sunflowers rock like epileptics

as bluejays ravage them,
      jabbing their shaggy heads.
            I met a scientist

who took me to his station.
      From nets as fine as filament,
            we plucked the wrens and warblers.

While he recorded data,
      I whispered secrets, some lies.
            I told a tanager her feathers

were the exact orange of a peach sorbet
      you once spooned into my mouth.
            The band on her leg said, "Remember."

You should see the crows,
      great thunderheads at dusk,
            roosting in our honey locust.

Your name is the song that's stuck
in their throats. They're sharpening
their beaks for your blue eye.

A Postcard from Heidelberg

The tourist city offers up its spaetzle
and beer, even at wobbly tables for one,
with sides of Gothic church and ruined castle.
I leave my euros, stroll as the evening sun
casts its gloss on cobblestones before
it sinks behind the walls. As if on cue,
a handsome man emerges through a door
and walks backwards into the avenue.
The street his orchestra, his pretty hands
rise and swing, conducting hearts in air.
Love can open windows in fairyland:
a woman leans out, arcs her own hands there.
He blows her kisses back, waves and whirls,
late for his shift, or to fuck some other girl.

My Father Takes Opium and Dreams of a Textile Mill

Machines pulled, pivoted and clacked
like oars of a great longship rowing to war.
They carded cotton through sharp metal teeth

that would take a man's finger if he nodded,
or bite the hand entire, spoiling the yarn
so he lost his day's wages as well as the hand.

Women ran the shuttles, breathing lint
like a damp, smothering rag held over their faces.
The doffers, barefoot boys in overalls,

swapped the bobbins full of new-spun thread
for empties, back and forth, ten hours,
twelve, fourteen. Dark, the windows bricked

for air conditioning never installed,
the windless air choked with sticky fibers,
the brown lung cough, the heat, no breeze or breath —

my father had a cough he couldn't shake.
His doctor prescribed a cherry syrup, which Dad
swigged without measuring. Days he managed,

driving somehow the half-mile to work
and back, but evenings at home, he gulped the codeine
until he lost time, lost himself.

He remembered the phone. "Where are we?" he asked his friend.
A joke, he thought at first — both men hated
the little Georgia town. "That's right — nowhere!"

By the time I arrived, Dad
had been discharged, still dehydrated
and weak enough that he endured my scolding.

He slumped in a chair, sipping Gatorade,
and watched me sort rancid, expired food
from the shelves of his fridge, scrub his crusted oven.

"I didn't know what day it was, or where
I was," he confessed. "I thought I worked
in a textile mill in North Carolina."

"Why?" I knew his father had been a welder,
building Southern dams for the TVA.
"Did anyone in your family ever work

in a mill like that?" He shook his head. The dream,
I saw, still frightened him. "I don't know why."
He studied the eerie neon blue in his glass,

as if sugar water could reveal
another life, a boy kept out of school
to earn a wage, a few dollars a week,

paid to a father with a missing pinky finger
and scarred lungs. Was he the doffer boy,
or the man who prayed for him? Which was worse?

That was years ago. Then he died.
If I could pray, I'd pray that he is nowhere,
a clean, empty space untouched by dream.

Once

Once, I found myself lost in a wood —
not an allegorical wood, but real
forest, oak, and loblolly pine,

probably owned by a lumber company
biding its time. I wandered down the paths
worn by whitetails. The sun fell behind

a stand of poplars. I had no bars, and soon,
no battery. The ardent peepers sang
all night; the moon and I hummed along.

It was rather nice to be alone, and so
I did not rush or panic. I licked the dew
from magnolia leaves. I ate seven toadstools

the color of napalm, and did not die. My hair
grew long as Spanish moss, and I brushed it smooth
with a comb of bones. Why cry out, or try

to find a way to leave, when everything
I needed was there? No one missed me, or sent
a search party. Perhaps I was not lost

at all, but came by choice. I slept on a bed
of ferns. Oh, the smell of the cooling earth!
Oh, the softness pushing through my back,

curling intimately through my jaw,
enfeathering the bird bones of my ear!
A red fox made off with my tibia,

but I did not begrudge it. He was a fox.
I like to tell this story on summer nights,
when owls cruise above on soundless wings.

Remember, every word of this is true.

Notes

"The Story of the Flood" is indebted to N.K. Sandars' excellent translation of *The Epic of Gilgamesh*.

"In the Castle of H.H. Holmes": For information on Herman Mudgett, also known as H.H. Holmes, the author is indebted to the documentary film *H.H. Holmes: America's First Serial Killer* and *The Devil in the White City* by Erik Larson.

"Balthus, *The Victim*, 1946" is inspired by the painting *The Victim* by Balthasar Klossowski, known as Balthus.

"*Action Comics* #0" references characters created by Jerry Siegel and Joe Shuster for D.C. Comics.

"Miss Emma Borden Visits Her Sister in Jail," "The Chauffeur's Daughter Recalls Miss Borden," and "Lizzie Borden's Pears": Several books, articles, and web sites contributed to the research for these poems. Especially helpful were *The Trial of Lizzie Borden*, edited by Edmund Pearson; *Women Who Kill* by Ann Jones; *Popular Crime: Reflections on the Celebration of Violence* by Bill James; and the web site *Lizzie Borden: Warps and Wefts* by Shelly Dziedzic.

The poems in section two take many of their titles and epigraphs from William Shakespeare's *Hamlet*. Allusions to and language from that play are also incorporated into many of the poems. "The Name of Action" takes its epigraph from T.S. Eliot's "The Love Song of J. Alfred Prufrock." "Questions" takes its epigraph from Tom Stoppard's *Rosencrantz and Guildenstern Are Dead*.

The Author

Juliana Gray is the author of *The Man Under My Skin* (River City Publishing, 2005) and *Roleplay* (Dream Horse Press, 2012), which won the 2010 Orphic Prize, as well as the chapbook *Anne Boleyn's Sleeve* (Winged City Press, 2014). Her poems have appeared in *Best American Poetry*, *Birmingham Poetry Review*, *Sou'wester*, *32 Poems*, and other journals and anthologies. An Alabama native, she lives in Alfred, New York, where she is a professor of English at Alfred University.